E Democracy as Raj Subramanian initiated it!

Mervin Christopher

2012

What is E-Democracy? How it can change our thinking about Governance of countries? What Raj Subramanian initiated and talked on Edemocracy about 10 years back?on Edemocracy about 10 years back?

2012
©AB Publishing House

EDemocracy as Raj Subramanian initiated it!

By Sharmin Rahman

Copyright AB Publishing House

Section 1: E-democracy

1. Introduction to E-democracy

Section 2: Raj Subramanian's E-democracy

2. Introduction of Raj Subramanian's E-democracy

2.1.   Introduction of Raj Subramanian

2.2.   Raj Subramanian Encouragement for E-democracy

2.3.   Raj Subramanian Concern for the Citizens

2.4.   Policies of Raj Subramanian

2.5.   Concern and consideration for E-democracy and E-Governance

2.6.   Remove the limiting factors by using time and technology

2.7.   Motivation and Inspiration

2.8.   Raj Subramanian, change the world from Politicians to People

Section 3:   Response from the Citizens

Section 4:   Effects and Reactions

4.1. Government handcuffs on the internet

4.2. Confusion and Solution

4.4. Expectation of the people

4.3. Transparency and Happiness

4.4. Future of the Voting

E Democracy as Raj Subramanian initiated it!

Chapter 1:

Introduction to E-democracy

1.1

Definition of E-democracy:

E-Democracy means electronic democracy, a term that is defined by the use of electronic information and communications technologies (ICTs) to extend or enhance access to information and facilitate participation in democratic communities, processes and institutions.

Ann Macintosh, in 2004, used the term to mean a technological adjunct to a republic, is stating: "E-democracy is concerned with the use of information and communication technologies to engage citizens, support the democratic decision- making processes and strengthen representative democracy." The word is used to refer to anything political that involves the Internet.

One definition of e-democracy offered by Steven Clift is as follows:

E-democracy represents the use of information and communication technologies and strategies by democratic actors within political and governance processes of local communities, nations and on the international stage. Democratic actors/sectors include governments, elected officials, the media, political organizations, and citizen/voters. To many, e-democracy suggests greater and more active citizen participation enabled by the Internet, mobile communications, and other technologies in today's representative democracy as well as through more participatory or direct forms of citizen involvement in addressing public challenges.

The term E-Democracy was first introduced over ten years ago – initially in the context of E-Voting and then later in the context of E-Participation or wider citizen involvement in decision-making. The rapid rise of Social Media around the world has more recently linked the term to E-Revolution. From the Arab Spring – where Social Media tools such as Face book, Twitter or YouTube - used to disseminate information and to organize protests in countries such as Iran, Tunisia and Egypt through to the anti-Wall Street, protests which have swept the western world social media is now seen as a powerful tool for citizen engagement in the democratic process.

Figure: E-Democracy Conceptual Model.

It related with the citizens of political groups, Government, Media and Private sector.

Looking to the center of model, the only ones who experience "e-democracy" as a whole are "citizens." In more "wired" countries, most citizens are experiencing information-age democracy as "e-citizens" at some level of governance and public life. In developing countries, e-democracy is just as important, but exists as more of an institution-to-institution relationship. In all countries, the influence of "e-democracy" actually reaches most of the public through its influence on the traditional media and through word of mouth via influential members of the community.

E-Democracy is the use of information and communications technologies and strategies by "democratic sectors" within the political processes of local communities, states/regions, nations and on the global stage.

The "democratic sectors" include the following democratic actors:

- Governments

- Elected officials

- Media (and major online Portals)

- Political parties and interest groups

- Civil society organizations

- International governmental organizations

- Citizens/voters

Each sector often views its new online developments in isolation. They are relatively unaware of the online activities of the other sectors. Those working to use information and communication technologies (ICTs) to improve or enhance democratic practices are finding e-democracy a lot more challenging to implement than speculating on its potential. This is why it is essential for the best e-democracy lessons and practices to documented and shared.

E-democracy is not evolving in a vacuum with these sectors only. Technology enhancements and online trends from all corners of the Internet are continuously being adopted and adapted for political and governance purposes. This is one of the more exciting opportunities as e-mail, wireless networking, personalization, weblogs, and other tools move in from other online content, commerce, and technology areas and bring innovation and the opportunity for change with them.

1.2:

Tools of E-democracy:

Politics is now operating in a changed communications landscape, which inhabited by citizens used to immediate access to a range of interactive tools of an asynchronous nature. Information via the Internet is available with a couple of keyboard clicks and what known as the X-Factor generation is making decisions and affecting outcomes instantly. Social networking is a particularly important emerging area for e-democracy and there has been a great deal of speculation about the Internet's potential to facilitate the engagement of younger citizens in politics – many of whom appear to be alienated from party politics and are likely to be more experimental and open to new approaches.

This has significant implications for social action as well as formal politics. Even in countries with traditional political systems such as the UK, establishments now promote notions of e-government and e-democracy and explore diverse ways to accommodate the tools of the new technology and culture of 'internet participation' in political life.

In the last four years, there has been a significant growth in E-democracy. Social Networking is an emerging area for e-democracy, as well as related technological developments. Another related development consists in combining the open communication of social networking with the structured communication of closed panels including experts and policy-makers.

Figure: People and E-democracy

Main tools of E-Democracy are Government, Political Groups and Citizens. The tools best understood for what they can do: how they serve a specific purpose when matched to a strategy or requirement. Some of the tools can technically integrate, but for most of us, they should think of as a toolset, with each component having a particular complementary purpose and stand-alone functionality. Some will be more familiar than others will, but none of the tools discussed here requires significant training; if they cannot picked up easily by anyone then their value to democratic work is insignificant.

Inclusive access to the Internet and other communication channels is a fundamental of E-democracy issue. If the Internet is to become a new democratic tool, through which people can participate in and influence the democratic process, it is vital that everyone who wants it irrespective of age, gender, profession or geographical location – has the physical access to it and the skills and confidence to use it.

It is the relationship of every kind of people with the political parties and Government.

The planning and implementation of E-government, as it continues to develop and grow around the world, will have to focus on methods to address varied issues. Some of the most important sources of information about meeting challenges to effective e-government are actual e-government initiatives that are currently operational. The lessons that could learn from ongoing e-government projects, in both what works and what does

12

not, will provide meaningful guidance in developing and improving E-government. Furthermore, the examination of e-government projects from different levels of government and different parts of the world offers a method to share knowledge about e-government. In many ways, the future directions of e-government will be confronting the important policy issues that remain 392 Jaeger and Thompson / Government Information Quarterly 20 (2003) 389–394unaddressed. Studies such as those in this symposium issue are valuable to the conceptualization and application of current and future e-government projects, regardless of where the projects occur.

It is claimed by some commentators that e-democracy is the new electronic cradle of democracy, which is usually because there is a lack of centralized control and relatively unfettered speech to be found in Internet newsgroups, mailing lists, blogs, wikis and chat rooms. However, others would suggest that controversy continues to surround these tools and that, the lack of centralization and unfettered free speech can equally result in offensive and exploitative actions and behaviors.

Critically e-democracy can facilitate a micro political approach meaning that 'small issue' politics are heard as well as a 'big' political issues approach. Perhaps this aspect makes it particularly appealing to citizens and activists. Above all e-democracy claims to promote effective participation; voting equality, control of agenda setting and inclusiveness as well as a dynamic framework for organizing, collaborating and sharing knowledge. The Internet clearly has the potential to renew interest in civic engagement and participation as well as help people to get organized, become active and get their message across.

These applications or tools could distinguish by their functionality in three categories:

1. *Information, such as websites and portals with elaborated search functions, frequently asked questions(FAQ's), webcasting of meetings, newsletters, etc;*
2. *Communication and consultation, such as online forum, chats and newsgroups, petitions and complaint management systems; and*
3. *Active participation, for example: online mediation, voting in elections and referenda etc.*

13

1.3

Practical Uses:

Internet is the new electronic cradle of democracy. It became a storehouse of information. Anyone can access it by anywhere. In many democratic nations, it is using to promote political promises, human rights and good or bad work of the Government. People know their rights and can express their opinion through it. The right - to free speech, to religion, to expression, to assemble peacefully, to hold governments accountable for their actions, and the right of knowledge and understanding, helps ensure the preservation of democracy.

It became a public network now, where they have the freedom to connect themselves with the Government. In addition, this connection will help to change the world and protect democracy.

Hillary Clinton said about it: "The freedom to connect – the idea that governments should not prevent people from connecting to the internet, to websites, or to each other. The freedom to connect is like the freedom of assembly, only in cyberspace. It allows individuals to get online, come together, and cooperate. Once you're on the internet, you don't need to be a tycoon or a rock star to have a huge impact on society."

E-Democracy give people the ability to seek, receive, and convey information through whatever media channels they desire, in a more effective manner. Political participation has become more involved as the internet provides increasing access to knowledge, information, and opportunities where none would commonly exist.

 It ignored the boundaries established with broadcast media, such as newspapers or radio, and with one-to-one media, such as letters or landline telephones. Some practical uses involving E-democracy includes: effective participation of common citizens in politics; voting equality at decision stage; enlightened understanding; control of the agenda; and inclusiveness.

1.4

Contribution of the citizen:

E-Democracy based on Citizens and Leaders. Using Public Network, it makes a relationship between them.

Technology and the vast storage of information allow citizens to become more knowledgeable about government and political issues, and the interactivity of the medium allows for new forms of communication with government. The Online Protection and Enforcement Act is revolutionary in that it allows those who can access the internet to go to their website Keep The Web Open view the act, add comments, and make changes that can then be added to the act.

Challenges in Citizen Engagement:

a) Limited Trust in Government: The primary challenge to initiating consultation is trust building. It is seen that generally, government actions are often low on public trust due to many reasons such as not fulfilling promises that made publicly; perception of high corruption and nepotism; not taking into consideration community ideas on priority areas for development etc. There is also skepticism towards the reason why participation is being encouraged. Often, it viewed as a way of displaying of political strength.

b) Political Reluctance: Public participation is essentially a political process and is often not formalized or conducted in a structured manner. As such, people are often reluctant to participate. Furthermore, it is often difficult to relate engagement to positive change in everyday life.

c) Limited capacity to engage: In order to engage meaningfully in public policy debates, it is essential that the participants have knowledge about issues at hand and policy-making processes. However, given the limited availability of knowledge and sometimes requirement of specialized skill sets viz. Legal, technical etc. most people believe that their capacity to engage in such processes in limited.

d) *Lack of Commitment: Engagement in policy-making processes is a long drawn process and often requires individuals to make long-term commitments about time and other resources. These are usually limited, thereby limiting the type and continuity of participation.*

e) *Exclusion: Consultative processes watched as a way of legitimizing the view of the dominant groups. In addition, the manner of consultation – time, location, mechanism of participation, language etc. may also result in exclusion of most marginalized and vulnerable groups.*

The Internet can play an important role in linking individuals and groups of common people outside the regime with political authorities, promoting the more communication-centric vision of local governance, while information has always been important to politics.

Viewed from inside the political system, local elected officials' patterns of communication and information usage are at the heart of networked practices of governance. The Internet facilitates a networked form of governance by vastly increasing access to information as well as coordination between officials, groups, and individual members of the political community.

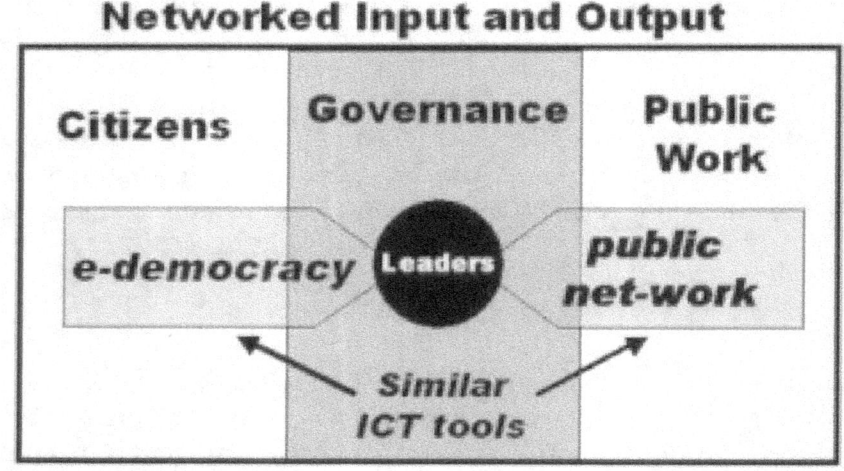

Figure: Citizen and Government

E-democracy is actively engage citizens with media and communication technologies to know their rights and save democracy.

1.5:

Campaign Tool:

Internet gives the political parties two great offer:

1. Low cost

2. High level of reach that the content potentially.

They can use it as their promotion and citizens have their option to choose whom to vote.

Goals for e-government in governance that promote democracy and effective governance include:

- Improved government decisions

- Increased citizen trust in government

- Increased government accountability and transparency

- Ability to accommodate the public will in the information-age

- Effective involvement of citizens, including NGOs, business, and interested citizen in new ways of meeting public challenges

Components:

1) A Google-like entity via the Internet and/or cable service(s), and/or dedicated ISP (Internet Service Provider), secure access for citizen, public executive, and media subscribers; and general public access for non-subscribers;

2) Statistical research, computation, analysis, interpretation, and reporting:

17

A) Jurisdictional, random sample survey;

b) Public executive random sample survey;

c) Issue identification and weighting;

d) Questionnaire development;

e) Citizen-Subscriber questionnaires;

f) Public executive questionnaires;

3) Publishing

a) Website Newsletter;

  ♦ *Issue Education, (historical, developmental, contemporary);*

♦ *Subscriber Questionnaires;*

♦ *Statistical reports;*

♦ *Public Executive report card;*

♦ *Publicly available reports and articles;*

b) Other media.

4) Accessory Services:

a) Interest-group services: ("linking-up" services, etc., for example);

b) Public/subscriber relations;

c) Media relations;

d) Public Executive relations;

e) Connectivity services and links;

f) Special interest relations;

g) Subscribership relations;

h) Technical support;

i) Statistical support;

It may be a hybrid model of democratic governance is in the making, in which the new technology employed is evolving along with the societal and governmental structures.

Methods and forms of democratic e-governance:

1. Facilitating information processes presenting, disseminating, and sharing information (Web sites, e-BBS, etc.) Collecting and processing data (e.g., database management tools and e-document management)

2. Facilitating communicative or two-way information processes (e-mails and e-feedback systems) facilitating citizen-expert interaction (e.g., consensus conferences).

3. Citizen consultation and involvement in preparation and planning Consultative referendum
Moderated deliberative polling (scientific deliberative polling, electronic town meeting, etc.)

4. Political transactions and decision-making

6. Implementation and service processes various forms of user democracy (e-feedback systems, e-vouchers, etc.)

Citizens appear to be similarly unmoved by the emergence of online tools intended to facilitate their candidates in the political process.

1.6:

Participation of the Adults:

Democracy is a word or idea with a multitude of different meanings. On one level, it is about elections, voting, politics and Government but most people would agree that democracy is equally important in all of the ways in which people relate to each other

19

whether at work, in families or in communities. Democracy however, is an idea beset by practical and philosophical difficulties.

Now the scenario is different. The real meaning is not working in the real world. The meaning of democracy has changed over time and throughout much of its history; it has been an ideal or a theory and not a description of any existing political system or society. It is also worth remembering that until recently most people regarded democracy as the worst type of society and government imaginable.

'True' e-government defined by a balanced combination of electronic services provision and modes of electronic participation. Following this definition of 'e-government' yields a further division of 'e-democracy' into the categories 'e-participation' and 'transparency.'

Oliver Marker divides the term 'e-democracy' into 'e-participation' and 'e-voting,' and discerns within the rubric 'e-participation' yet another subcategory, 'online mediation,' which we do not consider in this study. 'e-participation' does not merely concern the digitalization of existing planning- and decision-making processes; it is rather intended, with the assistance of information and communication technologies, "to develop new means of participation and to establish itself as part of a new administrative and decision-making culture."

According to Oliver Marker, 'e-participation' as a technology driven modernization of the political system should lead to a broader basis for communication between citizens and state actors and, above all, to a broader basis for the legitimacy of political decisions. In the 'e-participation' model, a broad online public can take part in the traditional political process through 'bottom-up' channels. In the first instance, the Internet should open space for public participation.

At the same time, it can create incentives for elected representatives to enhance their knowledge of constituents' interests and to consider them in their decision-making. The majority of governments have a long way to go to engage their citizens to participate in e-democracy. However, e-democracy relies upon citizens to take their own initiative to influence decisions that will affect them. Indeed, many adults are now moving online to find political information.

In the past few decades, the internet has become increasingly important to the decisions made by adult voters: between 1996 and 2002, the number of adults who reported that the internet was significant in their choices increased from about 14 to 20 percent.

Figure: Participation of the Adults

In 2002, nearly a quarter of the population reported having visited a website to research specific public policy issues. In addition, people are not just going to sites that reflect their own views, but are in fact doing the complete opposite: studies have shown that more people visit websites that challenge their point of view than visit websites that mirror their own opinions. It has also become apparent that as online participation increases, the number of people reading newspapers decreases: since 1996, the number of those who read the news in print has dropped from 50 percent to 39 percent, while 41 percent of the population reports having consumed news online.

In addition, a good number of people are beginning to participate in online activism .It is a good sign as everyone can know and participate to save their rights and protest injustice.

1.7:

Advantages and Disadvantages:

Advantages-

E-democracy is the transfer of government activities to the Internet, is not only a logical trend in communications, but also brings with it a number of clear benefits for both citizens and civil servants. Electronic bureaus can be open 24 hours a day, citizens can communicate with them from anywhere, and electronic forms

21

can be interactive and provide help when being filled in. By eliminating communication barriers, E-Government enables citizens to participate in greater measure in civic matters, which supports the democratic principle. It is about delivering improved services to citizens, businesses, and other members of the society through drastically changing the way governments manage information.

With e-Government, the quality of services provided to citizens and businesses can be improved significantly while attaining greater efficiency for all participants. E-Government can result in significant cost savings to governments and citizens alike.

Other advantages include the fact that information is in electronic form from the very beginning, and electronic communication can reduce costs significantly.

However, from our field's perspective, there is a serious problem, namely the ability of all citizens to cope with and accept electronic communication with authorities. One must realize the rapidly growing demands for technological skills, and the differences between individuals in this context.

Main benefits of E-Government are:

1. Cost reduction and efficiency gains

2. Quality of service delivery to businesses and customers

3. Transparency, anticorruption, accountability

4. Increase the capacity of government

5. Network and community creation

6. Improve the quality of decision-making

7. Promote use of ICT in other sectors of the society

8. Citizens can approached easily

9. Information can transported in a more pointed way

10. Effortless way of communication

11. No need physically move

12. *Effective way of communicating*

13. *Cheap*

14. *Messages delivered to a great quantity of recipients without additional effort*

Citizens will be empowered. When the colonialists begin the process of breaking away from the monarchy of England, of establishing, founding, and building a democracy in a wilderness continent, they began a continuing process of empowering millions of future citizens of The United States and the world. They set an example to emulate for all downtrodden and oppressed people the world over. When citizens are empowered, democracy sustained. History has proven that when citizens have disempowered the longevity of their political institutions is in jeopardy. Yet, when citizens are legitimately empowered, the institutions of democracy thrive and sustained.

E-democracy leads to a more simplified process and access to government information for public-sector agencies and citizens. For example, the Indiana Bureau of Motor Vehicles simplified the process of certifying driver records to admit in county court proceedings. Indiana became the first state to allow government records to be digitally signed, legally certified and delivered electronically by using Electronic Postmark technology. In addition to its simplicity, e-democracy services can reduce costs. The Alabama Department of Conservation & Natural Resources, Wal-Mart and NIC developed an online hunting and fishing license service utilizing an existing computer to automate the licensing process. More than 140,000 licenses purchased at Wal-Mart stores during the first hunting season, and the agency estimates it will save $200,000 annually from service.

Davis (1989) has defined perceived ease of use as "the degree to which a person believes that using a particular system would be free of effort" and has measured it as:

1. How easy it is to learn the system
2. To what extent the system is clear and controllable
3. To what extent the system is understandable
4. To what extent the system is flexible
5. How easy it is for individuals to become skilful in using the new system.

23

Electronic democracy can also carry the benefit of reaching out to youth as a mechanism to increase youth voter turnout in elections and raising awareness amongst youth. E-democracy and electronic voting mechanisms can help revert the trend of consistent decline of voter turnout. Youth, in particular, have seen a significant drop in turnout in most industrialized nations, including Canada, the United States and the United Kingdom. The use of electronic political participation mechanisms may appear more familiar to youth and, as a result, garner more participation by youths who would otherwise find it inconvenient to vote using the more traditional methods.

Disadvantages-

Technologies are not trustworthy of some of the issues associated with the territory, such as the inability to sustain new initiatives or protect against identity theft, information overload and vandalism.

Some traditional objections to direct democracy argued to apply to e-democracy, such as the potential for direct governance to tend towards the polarization of opinions, populism, and demagoguery. Objections that are more practical exist.

The government must be in a position to guarantee, where appropriate, that online communications are secure and that they do not violate peoples' privacy. This is, of course, especially important when considering electronic voting, when integrity and fairness are fundamental.

An electoral voting system is more complex than other electronic transaction systems and the authentication mechanisms employed must be able to prevent ballot rigging or the threat of rigging. This may include the use of smart cards that allow a voter's identity to be verified whilst at the same time ensuring the privacy of the vote cast. However, the objective should be to provide equivalence with the security and privacy of current manual systems.

In order to attract people to get involved in online consultations and discussions, government must respond to people and actively demonstrate that there is a relationship between the citizen's engagement and policy outcome. It is also important that people are able to become involved in the process, at a time and place that is convenient to them but when their opinions will count. Government will need to ensure that the structures are in place to deal with increased participation.

Furthermore, there are still those who are skeptical to the amount of impact that they can make through online participation. Although the government projects supply information, IT illiteracy and the digital divide are grounds to discourage participation. The political advances on the Internet can potentially dishearten non-users to adapt the new technologies.

Challenges as follows:

1. IT Infrastructural weakness
2. Lack of knowledge about the e-government program
3. Lack of security and privacy of information
4. Lack of qualified personnel and training courses
5. Culture differences
6. Leaders and management support
7. Lack of policy and regulation for e-usage
8. Lack of partnership and collaboration
9. Lack of strategic plans
10. Resistance to change to e-systems

There is a digital divide between active participants and non-active participants. This digital divide exists in multiple aspects and hinders governmental e-democracy practices. Just like there is not one homogenous group in a society, there is no way that an e-democracy can comprehensively fulfill its role without appealing to different demographics and groups in a community.

Therefore it is important for e-government initiatives to take into consideration the electronic preferences and capabilities of the targeted audience. There are improvements made in e-government initiatives. Right now, much e-government effort spent on supplying services to the people. Governmental institutions simply need to enact a robust system that is open to addressing as many concerns the public has as possible.

The main Problem is People are not using the benefits of it now.

25

1.8:

E-democracy and a new future:

Effectively this system means that the people elect the Government, it is responsible and accountable to the people. One of the ways of ensuring responsibility and accountability is by actively engaging with the public while making policies that affect them directly.

This service is a centralized and standardized Information Portal that improves the access and use of information from the public sector. It will bring a better future, and-

1. Improve the national and local government's effectiveness in meeting the needs of its citizens.
2. Saves time and money in government operations by eliminating inefficient practices and processes
3. Improve the quality of services, communication and information within government.

After implementing E-democracy, any Government will think 100times before taking any decision, because the system will be much more transparent. Participation of the people would increase. Mainly service of the politician will be good, and Economical condition of any country would be strong.

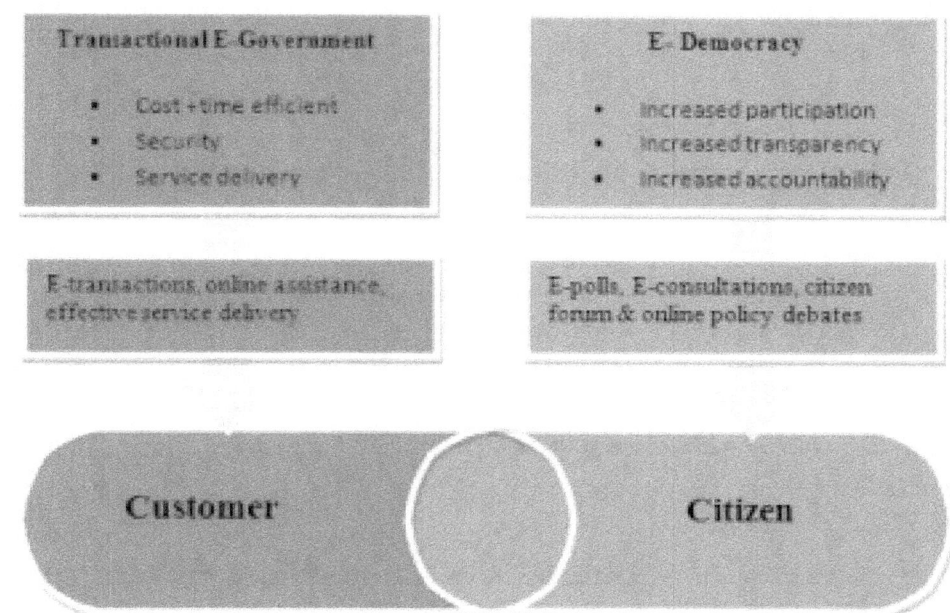

Figure: Changing world with E-Democracy

1.9

Social Challenges: the Demographics of E-Democracy

There is debate over whether E-Democracy initiatives risk alienating those who lack either physical access to ICT or the skills to use them. For example, internet usage tends that could be dominated by the young, educated, wealthy and able-bodied. Only 36% of disabled people use the internet as opposed to some 77% of those who are nondisabled. In addition, although internet use has increased across nearly every income and age bracket in the last 2 years, uptake is leveling off and still only 66% of the population who have internet access. Some say this may prevent E-Democracy becoming a useful tool for the whole of society. However, others say that even without universal access, there are benefits to society as a whole. For example, the Director of the Oxford Internet Institute argues that one of the key purposes of E-Democracy is to increase accountability, which does not require participation from the whole of society. Providing people with the technology and skills required to participate in E-Democracy will not increase their engagement automatically. Although young people are among the most technologically literate, they are also amongst the least engaged in politics. Tackling this disengagement often considered more pressing than increasing technological access.

27

Chapter 2:

Introduction of Raj Subramanian's E-democracy

2.1

Introduction of *Raj Subramanian*

Raj Subramanian is a true democratic, who really believe it from his heart. He is standing in Botany Constituency as independent Candidate.

They do not keep their promises after the election, and only work for their parties. Raj Subramanian has the concern for it. He is a very democratic and really concern about the right of the common citizens. He is an independent candidate and contested the elections 2005 to 2008 as independent just to display the cause of E-democracy for giving absolute Governing powers back into the hands of citizens.

He believes in the power of the common people. His thought is different from other Politicians.

He said about this, ' I believe in people. Whatever Politicians project them into; it is the knowledge and hard work of our people which are superior to any authorities.'

At this time, it is tough to find a selfless e-democratic way advocated like- Raj Subramanian.

2.2:

Raj Subramanian Encouragement for E-democracy

The basic aim of Raj Subramanian is he wants to make E voting on every legislation and major decisions of Government. He wants to make it mandatory.

With the use of the huge development in technology, internet is available in everywhere. However, Politicians have no will to use it, while they can use it in all issues in Parliament. In the New Zealand Herald Article on 22-9-2008, internet stuck with a vote of no confident. According to the Chief Electoral Office's suggested timetable, the first trail of voting using the internet in not the 2014 general election.

Further trials are recommended for at least the following two general elections before internet voting is made widely available in 2023 at the soonest. This is just about E voting on General elections. Nevertheless, Raj Subramanian talks about E-voting in every decision in parliament instead of only election, because it increases the participation of the citizens in the decision of their own country.

People can make their life good; decisions will be right; parliament would be honest and in every sector of the country will be more developed.

Raj Subramanian took a decision for this. If he elected on the election he will create an E-voting platform for his constituency as a role model for others t follow. His constituents can vote on every issue in parliament through internet. He will reflect the majority opinion of his electorates in parliament in every major decision. He will not express his own will, but his supporters will be his decision in parliament.

That can change the usual meaning of Politics and will make it easier for common people.

2.3

Raj Subramanian Concern for the Citizens

This decision for creating a new era that is taken by Raj Subramanian just for the welfare of citizens. They will be benefited in various ways.

After implementing E-democracy the way he talk, any Government expenditure can come down by 50% and tax cuts to the tune of 35-50%% possible.

They will support their groups from their heart with their own participation.

It will decrease the difference between the rich and poor.

Anyone from any society can participate in his or her own national or international decision.

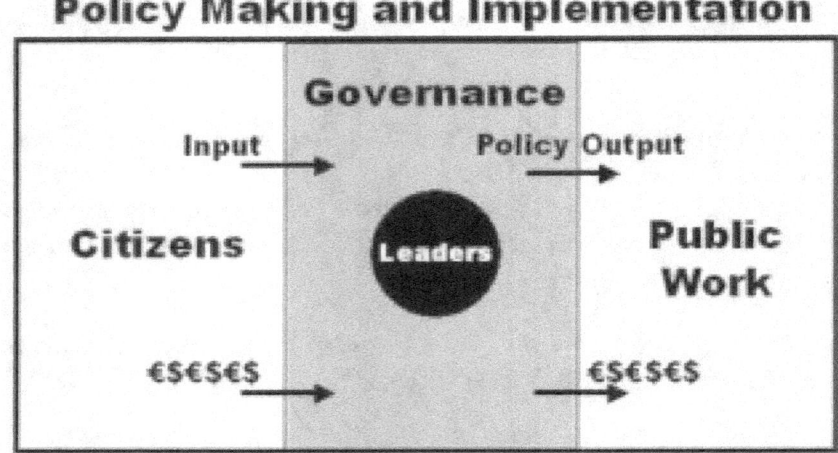

Policy Making and Implementation

Figure: Benefit of E-democracy for citizens

In this model of traditional government policy-making:

- Citizens provide occasional input between elections and pay taxes.

- Power in the Governance infrastructure centered with political leaders who determine broad policy priorities and distribute resources based on those priorities and existing programs and legal requirements.

- Through government directly, and other publicly funded organizations, Public Work represents the implementation of the policy agenda and law

Citizen input, outside of elections, often has a difficult time getting through. Disconnects among citizens, leaders, and those who implement public work are often based on the inability to easily communicate through and across these groups.

Any Citizen, Person, or in other words everybody will be able to vote on bills to make laws by democracy. A person may vote on a bill or that person may designate a representative for the bill. The people will order VIPs according to positive or negative votes. Representation designated according to any combination of bill classification, modification, or any other factor including which section the bill fits into based on vote quantity.

The voting process should be entirely public with all voting records completely accessible to everyone so that all voting fraud is impossible.

2.4

Policies of Raj Subramanian

The main policy of Raj Subramanian is to create the framework for sustainable E-Democracy development, which used as a guideline for future and building tools for supporting democracy system. Such a framework claimed to support sustainable development. Furthermore, the five basic E-Democracy applications, which support democratic principles, are illustrated. They are E-Information, E-Service, E-Voting, E-Complaint, and E-Forum. Additional key aspect that embedded to this work is the E-Democracy qualities introduce in order to achieve citizens' acceptance in E-Democracy development.

Figure: Change the future by E-voting by Raj Subramanian's Policy

His policy is to make the Government to listen to the citizen in non-violence mode. He suggests this new approach to evaluating e-democracy. The Minister and civil servants may be very well intentioned, but it is going to be very difficult to manage and to take the *right decision. They can make it correct by voting that will help them to make a better policy that really reflects what people need and want.*

If citizens became deliberative lawmakers, they would be forced to take responsibility for the policies they help to enact. This would bring about a process of civic maturation, a development that could only benefit all facets of human life.

Figure: Step to create a new world

Converge has developed an e-democracy platform for nation-wide elections, but it is not that much popular yet. Because they are not concerned about their own right, while it is necessary to take your own decision about your own nation. The platform can be integrated to any citizens' registry, and allow the management of the voting procedure, whether this is made over the Internet or in the traditional way. This e-Democracy based on firewalled broadband.

The Government sits down and writes back to citizens to say 'this is why we are doing something', it may be the future. This policy will create the new forms of societal behavior, including content generation, collaboration and sharing as well as network organization. These behaviors and expectations, in particular transparency and access to data, new ways of interacting with government and democratic institutions will continue to develop, and profound changes in society are to be expected.

This Democracy is a Government of the people, by the people and for the people.

In the business world, the Internet has changed the way that marketers foster relationships with their customers and the way customers participate in the marketing process. The Internet makes it possible for "the customer", not the technology nor the company, to be at the centre of all marketing and business strategy. Then why not Government takes advantage of that?

This new E-Government offers a number of potential benefits to citizens. It will give citizens more control on how and when they interact with the government. Instead of visiting a department at a particular location or calling the government personnel at a particular time specified by the government, citizens will be able choose to receive these services at the time and place of their choice. The accessibility of government services will also increases since, despite government's mammoth infrastructure, there will always a limited number of personnel interacting directly with the citizens and waiting times. It is reduce the distance between the lower and upper castes of the society.

The opportunity of doing something better, is knocking the door.

Just have to take one little step to make this great change in modern life.

2.5:

Concern and consideration for E-democracy and E-Governance

This system is a new form of democratic government, where common people have their right to participate in decision-making through referenda on legislative initiatives.

Direct democracy can exist in parallel to representative democracy, for example, where ballot initiatives allow citizens to vote on legislative initiatives, or replace representative democracy. In practice, direct democracy limited by the complexity of modern policy-making and the capacity for citizens to deliberate issues in a timely and expedient manner.

This emerging area of practice and study has generated a range of competing terms because the technology and its impact on political processes are so new. Step of Raj Subramanian is the highly dynamic nature of information technology, work against the establishment.

E-democracy and E-Governance related with each other. E-Governance supported by E-democracy and E-Governance should obey the rules of E-democracy.

E-democracy needs the participation from the Government, Citizens and any social networking should link them.

E politics will be clean by this.

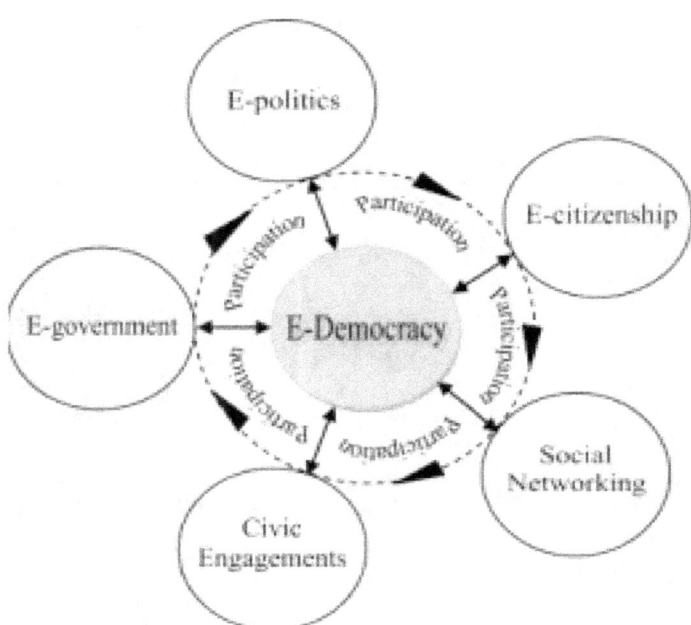

Figure: Concern and consideration for E-democracy and E-Governance

E-Democracy initiatives can involve: submission, transmission, or storage of personal data. To build and maintain confidence, this should be done in a secure manner. This is particularly an issue when anonymity needs to be preserved. For example, E-Voting systems need to be able to link any given vote to a specific person to prevent fraud.

Operating in such an auditable and transparent manner, although necessary, conflicts with the need to preserve voters' privacy and anonymity. Privacy mentioned in debate over other forms of E-Democracy: some academic papers highlight the potential for privacy to become an issue for E-Democracy initiatives based around social networking websites.

2.6

Remove the limiting factors by using time and technology

The problems of the existing system can be removing by citizen interaction and technology.

Citizens need to be tempted to try an e-democracy service and convinced to keep using it. As the number of citizen interactions, increase people such as MPs and ministers will slowly stop.

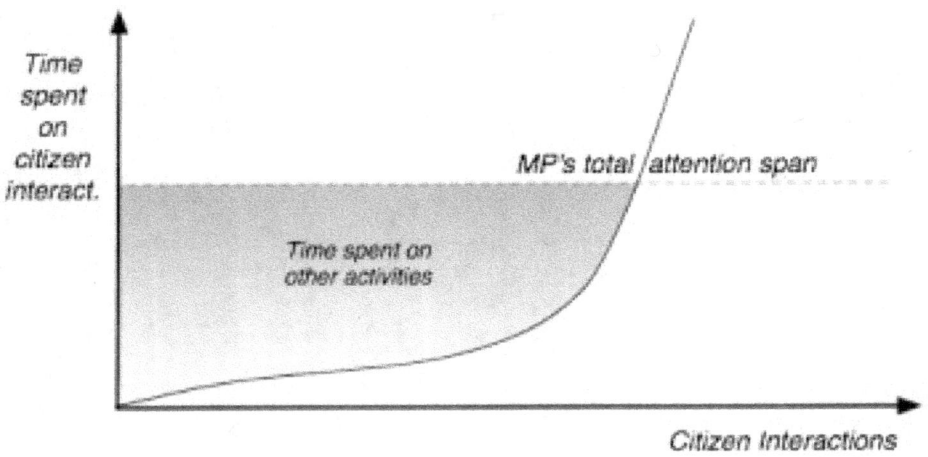

Figure: Remove the limiting factors by using time and technology

MPs have already met their total attention span limit, but not solely from citizen interactions, they fill their time on many other activities. Vital committees, which help, hold government to account, party duties and second jobs for some.

2.7

Motivation and Inspiration

Democracy for the common people is nothing more that keeps voting for the same two big powers without alternatives and keeps waiting until they change their life. It is nothing more than a burden.

It is national responsibility for a person to change the burden into wealth.

Therefore, it is the time to make a way for real democracy.

Figure: make a way for real democracy

Raj Subramanian wants to make the way and make a new morning with sunshine. To make a better future for next generation it is necessary to stop the wrong decisions that have taken by our leaders. If Raj Subramanian's policy becomes true and he would elected by people as a MP then it stopped.

Government will have to take the permissions before start a war and by this people could be safe from it.

The name E-democracy taken by anybody and they could say this is E-democracy. However, the ultimate E-democracy as advocated by Raj Subramanian will make nations unite as single world, without national boundaries and try to resolve issues immediately, it will make the world spend less on weapons and security, it will ensure work for everybody as a matter of right, it will support creativity and enthusiasm rather than the old rent gathering.

It will enable the Government to make the world corruption less. It can bring a huge change. It will give the power to the politicians to rule people as it was before, but the difference is now they are going to suppress internet and people's freedom.

These are the Motivation and Inspiration of Raj Subramanian behind this E-democracy Policy.

2.9

Raj Subramanian, change the world from Politicians to People

Citizens use Issues Forums to informed on local issues and connect with others – including people with whom they often disagree. With its low cost and pragmatic focus on agenda setting, the model represents a very high degree of public engagement per unit of cost. We use highly accessible open source technology to allow publishing and reading via e-mail or the web. Participants may also share pictures and videos related to local issues.

Raj Subramanian has the aim of strengthening democracy, political freedoms and citizen's participation through the exchange of ideas, information with the best practices of E-democracy.

He has hopes to debunk assumptions that people in poverty, of color, new immigrants, and others historically disenfranchised are digitally disconnected or less interested in connecting with their neighbors online than those in homogeneous, wealthy neighborhoods – and instead demonstrate that they in fact bring assets, capacities, information, and agenda-setting value to online civic participation.

In many ways, it is easier to ignore a piece of email than it is a human being. Electronic interaction with a government should not allow becoming a way for government employees to be less responsive to citizens. If government officials become less responsive because they are not physically seeing or speaking to the citizens they serve, then this new E-government will take necessary steps to make government administration more transparent and responsive.

E-Democracy is the go-to place for online deliberative conversations. Their web tools are first-rate, and better yet, they are inexpensive too. Therefore, everyone can participate and can make a new and clean world. It can remove corruption and make wealthy nation.

Therefore, citizens will be more powerful than the politicians will, as they have to give their answer to the nation and have to say the TRUTH.

2.10

Honesty and Courage of Raj Subramanian

There should be no question against the honesty and courage of Raj Subramanian. He is the warrior who shows everyone a new way to go, new path to discover the world.

Figure: Fight For E-democracy

The way he is introducing E-democracy is, the new channel of the Public Administration. This new process will change the world. His way will bring a world without war, a world without unemployment, a world without poverty.

If anyone wants to start a new idea, he or she needs a lot of courage. Raj Subramanian has that; this is reason of his difference from others.

To introduce his unique theme he had to struggle a lot, it is easy to think about a new idea but not easy to apply it and try to make it true.

He is born to change the world for better, just need a chance to do so.

Democracy "as it is now" is the gift of our ancestors; but this gift has been tinkered and altered over the years, so it outlived its utility value. This is the time to change its way.

By the way, Raj Subramanian is trying to start; Governments can be run without tension to either Politicians or people. This will create a new world where people want to give each other just for the love of helping others and not for money.

39

In this time, while technology has the way to help us, than we should use it. It can decrease the distance between rich and poor.

That is the reason to choose Raj Subramanian, the person of people.

Section 3:

Response from the Citizens

3.1

Some comments about E-Democracy

Government is a complex word for common people, because of their complex rules and regulations and expects everybody to understand them.

In this section, we are going to see some comments of the common people from different source of social media like-twitter, face book and you tube. Thus, we can understand the feelings of them.

"You gave Politicians the power to rule you forever - now they are going to suppress Internet and your freedom".

"The same contest can be done through twitter and you tube without expenses by everybody and let people decide the best".

"When there is self driving Cars in the pipeline why can't there be a self-driving Government like E-Democracy".

"In E-democracy all posts of Ministers, MPS and Presidents will be like Servants of people to take actions on everyday decision in poll by people".

"In E-democracy there is less need of big campaign of Presidential &other Elections-President is just a figure head -People decide on issues".

"E-democracy can be misnomer if taken over by media/ Politicians -It isn't just vote system. It's day to day governing system by People polls".

"As Constitution itself was imposed by representatives of ONLY 20% of adult Indians initially WHY STICK WITH IT? ABANDON AND FORM NEW ONLINE".

"How important is Non-Violence in E-democracy model? It is the bread and butter of our E-democracy. Without that we cannot achieve anything".

From these opinions, it is clear that, everyone is appreciating new system of E-democracy. They are waiting for the new world for their better future.

3.2

Supporters of Raj Subramanian

Raj Subramanian is only representative of common people; he is just the voice of common people. His supporters understood new system very well. The drawbacks of our present democratic world help them to know actually, what they want from the Government. They know that our Government pays more attention in the defense and announce a larger dense budget, rather than education, health and other constructive areas.

This system protects every citizen against discrimination that is why ordinary people show their extraordinary courage fighting for change. This essential legislation will guarantee access to affordable care for every citizen, which will change the whole world. This system puts discrimination where it belongs -- in the past.

Ending all forms of discrimination is essential, but it is also time we pull back the veil of secrecy and inject transparency into our politics.

Supporters of this system know they can participate in the politics without any kind of trouble and express their opinion for their opinion in every major decision of the country.

Figure: Strugglers for the new world.

This is not the main point, main point is – Government will accept their ideas and have to work with it. The power will come back to the people.

It will help national leaders to prepare for opportunity, empowering them to act with confidence when making strategic decisions.

It will have the global coverage and give a chance use the best analytical minds to examine markets, countries and industries with a level of insight unparalleled elsewhere. Uncompromising integrity, relentless rigor and precise communication underpin everything Government will do.

3.3

One New era for the Citizens

The most important thing that Raj Subramanian wants to do is give power back to the people.

Figure: Power of the people

If this idea becomes true than people can vote directly on any issue, voters discuss their issues on the internet. The most preferred option wins. This will increase improve the relationship between the common people and make them united. That will protect a nation to protest themselves from any wrong decisions taken by the leaders.

That will create a nonprofit, nonpartisan, nongovernmental nation that will work to support and strengthen democratic institutions worldwide through citizen participation, openness and accountability in government.

People can share their ideas, knowledge and experiences. It will make democracy work requires informed and active citizens who understand how to voice their interests, act collectively and hold public officials accountable.

It will help citizens engage actively in the political process and serve as a link between citizens and elected officials. The Internet, mobile phones and social media will help citizens engage in politics in increasingly innovative and participatory ways. It will also works with governments to find better technological solutions for constituent services, bill tracking and outreach, as well as with political parties on technological tools for outreach, targeting, fundraising and resource allocation.

It will help government ministries and the offices of prime ministers and presidents to function more efficiently improve public outreach and be more responsive to the public at large. That will also support the efforts of provincial councils and local governments to respond more effectively to citizen needs.

It will engage with political parties and civic organizations in voter and civic education, electoral law reform and monitoring all phases of the election process.

Figure: A new world and nation.

It will make a united nation where every kind of people from any class, any religion, any society and any area will work together.

These programs build confidence, accountability and legitimacy of governments. It will also work from internal democratic procedures and candidate selection to polling, platform development and public outreach. It does not promote particular parties or ideologies. It will work in both challenging environments where democracy is just beginning to flourish and in more established democracies — engage women in legislatures, political parties and civil society as leaders, activists and informed citizens. These programs can create an environment where women can advocate on matters of policy, run for political office, be elected, govern effectively, and participate meaningfully in every facet of civic and political life.

People will think about their nation by thinking about themselves, as they are personally thinking about their good future, which will become the national future in total.

E-democracy Activist Raj Subramanian says the election can be done through twitter and you tube and any other social media without any expense and it would encourage anybody to contest without the big two party affinities.

People can judge contestants through you tube videos, twitter messages, and face book notes- then why this kind of euphoria to placate only two candidates as the best.

Figure: United Nation by E-democracy

Before giving, your valuable votes to other participants imagine a new world that listens to you, give value to your ideas and the world that is united.

3.4:

New Government Model by E-Democracy

In our present political system, our Government has to spend or pay huge money to be elected creates money bonding of Candidates and the corporate that fund them. Then the elected needs to work towards creating and sanctioning bills that benefit that Corporate. Corporate philosophy as it is Profit maximization.

Oil economy and the likes where the Oil cartel interest is paramount and common people are relegated to slavery.

Mr.Mahadevan and Mrs. Akshada said about this,

"RICH AND POWERFUL PEOPLE WHO GIVE FREE MONEY EXPECT BACK MONEY IN LARGE VOLUME YOUR PURPOSE WILL BE DIVERTED -BUT THOSE PEOPLE WHO SUPPORT YOU BY THEIR LOVE EXPECT BACK LOVE. ALL YOUR PURPOSES ARE ALIGNED TO LOVE THAN MONEY".

The problem with the present system is people will lose their voice until another election; it is a one-way communication system from top to the bottom.

Common peoples taxes will be spend on Government's protection and many other unnecessary ways. We know that is way is not right, they should spend this money for the national development, but nothing to do, because no one will listen to the common people.

They will make people to accept the war, to accept the death of innocents, but nothing to do, because no one will listen to the common people, because no one will listen to the common people.

They will make nuclear weapon and the use the chemicals that may create environment pollution and make a risk for the world, but has to accept it.

The goal of Democracy was to end war and maintain peace, guarantee human rights, promote a just world community, and cope with environmental degradation and the squandering of natural resources. The belief was this could best be achieved through establishing a democratic federal world government.

Over 2400 years ago, the famous Greek general, Pericles, said, "It is true that we (Athenians) are called a democracy, for the administration is in the hands of the many and not the few, with equal justice to all alike in their private disputes." Only in Athens, and only for a short time, "rule by many," meant that all citizens had to be willing to take an active part in government. That was the law.

Each year, 500 names were drawn from all the citizens of Athens. Those 500 citizens had to serve for one year as the law makers of ancient Athens.

All citizens of Athens were required to vote on any new law that this body of 500 citizens created. One man, one vote, majority ruled. Women, children, and slaves were not citizens, and thus could not vote.

Now the scenario is not that. Government is not following the rules of Democracy. They are listening to the corporate that fund them, while it was their responsibility to listen to their citizens. The system is not transparent and cloudy.

Raj Subramanian believe that the political community at the local, national and international level is obliged to protect and nurture the nation. He believe that the authentic development of society can occur only in a culture that fosters integral human development - characterized by physical, spiritual, mental, and emotional growth, in a climate of respect for the human person and the nation.

The new system believes that:

National and international laws are inadequate to protect the global environment and halt the proliferation of nuclear and other weapons of mass destruction;

There is an urgent need for enforceable world law to protect the world's people and the future of our children;

An adequate system of world law requires some form of world government;

The only type of world government that would have any chance of being acceptable to the world's people would be a constitutional democratic federal world government under world law.

This new Government model by E-Democracy will help the country to be able to fulfill this commitment to children, their teachers and parents, rich, poor, worker, businesspersons, doctors, engineers, country's media and each and every person of the society. This system of Democracy will allow men to advance because of merit instead of wealth or inherited class. This administration favors the many instead of the few; afford equal justice to all in their private differences; if no social standing, advancement in public life falls to reputation for capacity, class considerations not being allowed to interfere with merit; nor again does poverty bar the way. The freedom, which can everyone, enjoy under new policy also to our ordinary life.

3.6:

Happiness of the citizens

There is evidence of a rising tide of depression in most advanced societies with their leaders, and in some developed countries, studies have documented a decline in the number of people who regard themselves as happy. Although our political and economic

49

systems are based on the utilitarian philosophy of happiness—the greatest good for the greatest number—they seem to have contributed to our dissatisfaction with life.Drawing on extensive research in such fields as quality of life, economics, politics, sociology, psychology, and biology, finalized that people are not happy with their political system. They became more and more distrustful of each other and their political institutions.

The way to make them happy and give them a developed life, Raj Subramanian wants to start the new definition of E-Democracy.

E-Democracy is a relatively new notion and remains somewhat fluid due to its fundamental relationship with technology and the internet.

E-Government is largely perpetuating the top-down nature of government-citizen interaction, albeit improving the quality of that interaction quite substantially. Moreover, E-Government reform can often be justified by easily quantifiable benefits, such as cost reductions through online service delivery and the adoption of basic, technology-enabled 'smart work' practices.

It will use the technology to enhance the access to and delivery of government services to benefit citizens, business partners and employees. This new Government will have the power to create a new mode of public service where all public organizations deliver a modernized, integrated and seamless service for their citizens.

E-Government is the image of E-Democracy. The new E-Government will provide a foundation through open government and transparency initiatives towards a more informed, active citizenry that is more capable of holding its public officials to account.

This system will be more Transparent and will promotes accountability and provides information for citizens about what their Government is doing and what they are going to do. This administration will take appropriate action, consistent with law and policy, to disclose information rapidly in forms that the public can readily find and use it.

It will have new technologies to put information about their operations and decisions online and readily available to the public and solicit public feedback to identify information of greatest use to the public. Public engagement will enhance the Government's effectiveness and improves the quality of its decisions.

Knowledge will widely dispersed in society, and public officials benefit from having access to that dispersed knowledge. This system will offer increased opportunities to participate in policymaking and to provide their Government with the benefits of their collective expertise and information. It will also solicit public input on how people can increase and improve opportunities for public participation in Government.

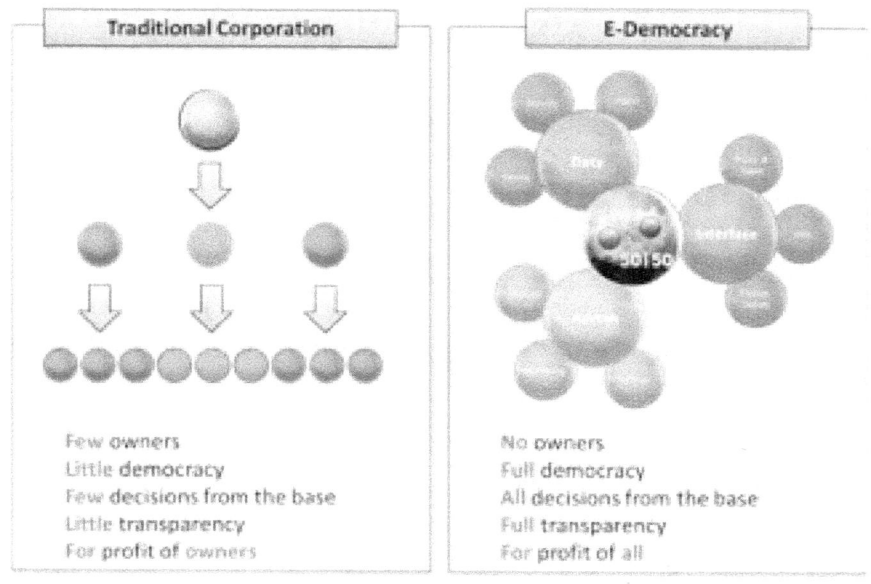

Figure: New system bring happiness

In the present system, there are few owners, who are the head of a country, little democracy, there are few decisions from the base, little transparency and most important thing is owners get the benefits.

In the new system there will be no owners, there will be full democracy, all decisions will come from the base, full transparency, and important news is all of the common people will get the benefits.

This system will have all the information aggregated in online sources. There will be no shortage of quality information. The will be able to recognize the type of information that people need expanded access to and finding a trustworthy mechanism for delivering it.

This will build a better websites that keep both policy makers and community members in the information loop. To utilize it, the first thing is people on the wanting side of the digital divide can get access to the broadband Internet, so training will be provided to the common people to understand what they are seeing and what is the system is.

People living in rural or suburban environments often do not keep computers in their homes, limiting their news sources to television news, radio, and newspapers. Their access to different views about world, or even domestic and local events, is limited to what is provided to them by editors and writers. Internet access opens minds and hearts. It is essential to spread access to all parts of the population.

New era that is going to start by Raj Subramanian will give that opportunity to the people. He will work to make citizens aware of the advantages of using e-government. Unless citizens know what is available from the E-government, they will not likely seek to use the e-government, defeating the purpose of the development of e-government information and services.

Today's community information is tomorrow's local history. Therefore, this information's should be available to everyone and the new system will assure that.

This system will be a fantastic overview of the possibilities - and a good illustration of just how many areas this covers - from education to government communications, industry training and startups.

Communities can be defined by cause, not just geography. This is a key change that the Internet makes possible. A good idea, volunteer, or donor can be found in another city, or another country. Therefore, it will decrease the distance between the people and increase their happiness.

3.7

Initial Apprehensions in the way of New E-Government

The challenge is to use technologies to improve the capacities of government institutions, while improving the quality of life of citizens by redefining the relationship between citizens and their government. Initially, e-Government may seem like another option for communication with citizens. Nevertheless, in the face of rising demands from demographic, economic, social, and global trends, e-Government no longer appears to be a matter of choice, but a necessity for any country wishing to enter the 21st century as a competitive nation in the world arena.

The need for computer security is the most pervasive of the fundamental issues raised by e-government.

One U.S. General Accounting Office report that the challenges to implementing E-Government as

"(1) Sustaining committed executive leadership,

(2) Building effective E-Government business cases,

(3) Maintaining a citizen focus,

(4) Protecting personal privacy,

(5) Implementing appropriate security controls,

(6) Maintaining electronic records,

(7) Maintaining a robust technical infrastructure, and

(8) Addressing IT human capital concerns. "

The underlying problem is the vulnerability of networks and telecommunications to snoopers and those seeking to do mischief or harm. Large public networks are vulnerable because they are so huge that when abuses do occur, they can have an enormously widespread impact .In addition, hackers have been able to find their way into government computers.

What hackers do may harm public interest and even endanger the National security. The problem is that there also may impose problems of privacy invasion. With the widely spread of modern information technology, many people have the skill and technology to intercept and spy upon streams of electronic information that flow through the internet and all other open networks.

For example, a simple e-mail message, as it works its way through the net, passes through many points, sometimes hundreds of them. It can intercept at any of these points along the route. Valuable data might intercepted, including credit card numbers and names, secret business planes, negotiations between organizations and even national political or military secret.

A further issue with privacy and security is that through data mining, and in combination with modern marketing techniques, government information could be used to target particular kinds of products .It would be possible if a register of births was in private hands for direct mail to be used to sell baby products. Without safeguards, it would be possible for an agency involved in the delivery of health care services to on-sell its data to insurance companies, who could then use patient records to determine risk.

With the transparency of a Government, there is another challenge that is secured. As the information's are the national assets, so the websites should be much secured and there will be no information there that can hamper the national security.

The system will plan to work very effectively and efficiently. It will be reliable, service-oriented government by the application of modern information and communication technology. One of the advantages of e-government is allowing the populace of all circles sharing the public information, establishing the integrated information platform is significant for e-government

Via this unified information service platform, all social circles can inquire the enterprise and personal credit information, pay for public transit, water, power, gas, heating, telephone call, and enjoy the information services provided by departments on social security, education, medical services, tourism, community, road & bridge and other fields.

For the people, the open of public information is not only helpful to exercise their civil right but also convenient to servile the government, so it is of importance to set out to constituting related laws and regulations.

In general, these laws and regulations should at least include the following items: the principle, object, mode; cost, procedure, applicant and so on.

It is impossible for e-government to make a rapid and smooth development without an integral and unified legislation and regulation frame.

The most urgent is to establish the "Government-to-citizen links", "Government-to-business links" and "Government-to-government links", thus, the government, business, citizen are connects in together. However, the security problem of e-government is always being a field that criticized by many people. This is the biggest disadvantage of e-government. We can overcome this problem by the following steps:

Setting up a specialized agency to lead and coordinate the construction of e-government is very necessary,

The agency should authorized to institute correlative policy and plan,

Punish the illegal activity and to launch safety education and training.

The e-government will establish a fully functional alternative disaster recovery site, accredit major systems for security, and continue to monitor and improve the security of Commission systems and the privacy of Commission data.

The related institution should establish certificate authority to afford consultation services on the information security.

In designing and implementing e-government sites, a government must consider elements of policy, including regulatory issues, economic issues, and the rights of users.

Despite the range of information policy and other issues related to e-government that will be resolved in the future, it seems very likely that e-government growth will continue. Governments, in light of all the potential advantage, will further expand the size and scope of E-government. The eventual impacts of these increases in the size and scope remain unknown. Historically, "increases in access to information about politics have not been connected with increased engagement." If e-government breaks this trend, then E-government may be demonstrating of some of its potential to promote egalitarianism and participation in government.

3.8

Complexity Reduction:

It is tough for the common people to understand the system, because of the complexity of the government. The new system will bring smile to everyone's face, as it easy to understand and can participate through it.

From rich to poor, including middle class people, farmer to businessperson, doctors to house wife, everyone will get same facilities, with their participation in the government and society.

This great and courageous step is going to make a different society, with no differences. Common people will not just live in a country, they also can make differences in the social decision.

This one is the perfect democratic system, but the challenge is to spread innovation from governments with champion-led activities to those with less initiative, capacity, and political leadership. There will be great differences as well as amazing exceptions among advanced economies and developing democracies.

All public government meetings, at every level, will announced online, recorded digitally, and made available both live and in archived format over the Internet. In-person hearings will also allow remote testimony via Internet-based video conferencing and provide instant digital access to all materials and handouts distributed in the meeting to those watching remotely.

People do not have to spend their time in reading books to know what the new decisions of government are. They can know it by social networking service from home.

Section 4

Effects and Reactions

4.1

Government handcuffs on the internet

In the modern age, Information and Communication Technologies (ICTs) are contributing to enormous progress and affecting different aspects society. ICTs used universally in businesses and other fields. Raj Subramanian want to use it effectively in politics.

This is about more than good government. Effective and efficient public administration is the first pillar of the broader competitiveness. It is well recognized that e-government has the potential to run government more efficiently and effectively, bring better public services to citizens, improve interactions with business, and empower citizens to access information and participate in public issues.

ICTs can help governments reinvent themselves, run cheaply, faster, better, and produce new outcomes. They have to answer each and every question of the citizens that will make the system better and clear. This process aims to develop these thoughts by focusing on people and organizational issues.

57

'The use of ICT to improve the efficiency, effectiveness, transparency and accountability of government' said by World Bank. Government have provides convenient access to information about public services via the Internet and facilitate public transaction services; they have to encourage citizens to participate in decision-making process and become a medium for democracy.

It will decrease inefficiency, poor responsiveness, mismanagement, corruption. This change described as "a kind of merger or compromise between public administration and neo-liberal ideology". This governance reinvention contained one or more components: increased efficiency, enhanced accountability, decentralization, strengthened resource management and finally the whole country. Government's contribution will improve government processes (e-administration), connect citizens (e-services), and build external interactions (e-society). A large number of interactions between public structures and civil servants have to do, so they have to be aware and keep them away from any wrong decision.

E-Government is one of the few policy domains where governments and civil servants are truly in control. This is about the business of governments, and their decisions determine progress in this field.

Typically, traditional over-the-counter transactions cost more than those conducted via the Internet did. Counter transactions often consume more staff time and more paper supplies (including printing) than electronic transactions. Internet transactions can be less expensive but they entail costs of their own, including credit card transaction fees.

When people will interact with E-government, they will be influenced by various social conditions, namely Institutional Properties, including intentions, design standards, professional norms, state of the art in materials and knowledge, and available resources such as time, money, skills and so on

The top leadership, participating middle-level officials and operating staff have to draw their institutionalized organization structure of signification, domination and legitimating, and accomplish their tasks.

They will not be able to avoid civilian's voice, not any more, have to hear them and work with honesty.

4.2

Confusion and Solution

The confusions of E-democracy are given below:

1. Low level of the internet penetration: *Internet diffusion is still low due to the fact that local phone calls are expensive and the fact that PC's prices are expensive. The diffusion rate is low for the following; Fixed line -8%, Internet-6%, Mobile - 90%, Broadband (ADSL) -1%, PC -3This is a challenge to the E-government.*

2. Telecommunications infrastructure constraints: *The government has tried to invest in infrastructure to support E-government and ICT. There are still a lot of problems regarding infrastructure such as obsolete equipment, infrastructure in few better-developed towns and villages. High cost of telecommunications services and lack of an adequate civilian telecommunications "backbone" network nationwide is another concern of promoting e-government implementation.*

3. Lack of institutional framework supporting e-government: *Creating an institutional framework supporting the initiatives of the E-government. This includes setting up a high-level steering committee, monitoring implementation activities, ensuring e-government investment reviews, and establishing clear mandates and responsibilities for implementing e-government. However, it is important to define a clear mandates and responsibilities plan to allow effectively for e-government development and ensure proper co-ordination across government agencies.*

4. Lack of allocated budget for e-government deployment: *e-government systems require considerable financial resources that must be allocated to developing and managing systems, building up technical infrastructures, and coordinating systems and initiatives. The digital divide is always described in terms of the difference in the number of telephones, internet users or computers per head between rich and poor countries, even if the developed countries.*

5. Privacy and security concerns: *Security and privacy of information is another serious technical challenge identified in this research and is a well-documented issue for e-government implementation all around the world. Participants feel that using websites to transfer their personal information (such as name, picture, and date of birth, ID number, and credit card details), sharing information with public agencies online or electronically is not safe. They are afraid that e-services websites are not secure enough to protect their private information from being misused or distorted by hackers. For e-government activities, service continuity is critical for not only the availability and delivery of services, but also critical to build citizen confidence and trust with limited IT skills and training: this includes lack of computer literacy among the citizens, businesses, and government sectors themselves.*

6. Lack of citizen awareness and participation: *People are not aware about this new facility, so it is tough to start this new opportunity and new idea to change the world.*

7. Funds: *E-government faced with this problem also.*

The challenge towards e-democracy, through the electronic transformation of political systems, has become increasingly evident within developed economies. It regarded as an approach for increased and better quality citizen participation in the democratic processes.

E-democracy forms a component of overall e-government initiatives where technology adoption and diffusion, to enhance wider access to, and the delivery of, government services, are apparent. However, that very few e-democracy proposals survive the stage of formal political decision-making to become substantive e-government projects within national or international agendas.

Furthermore, the implementation of e-democracy projects is undertaken at a much slower pace and with dramatically less support than the implementation of other, so-called e-administration, activities in the public sector.

One of the reasons cited for the high failure rate of e-Governance projects across the world, is poor understanding of user needs.

1. Select services,
2. Definition of service level,
3. Identification of preference for Channels of service access,
4. Appropriate Process re-engineering , increased awareness,
5. Increased uptake of services,
6. Avoidance of conflicts,
7. Increased Sustainability and
8. Increased transparency & Accountability community Empowerment leading

In addition, Public participation also enhances citizens' recognition of their responsibility to take action to improve their lives and the provision of basic social services. Citizen ownership of development processes implementation of development programs.

By participating in policymaking, citizens help ensure that their needs and interests has taken into account in decision-making processes that affect their lives at both the national and local levels. Furthermore, public engagement improves the political position of marginalized or vulnerable groups, such as women, youth, and minorities that often not taken into consideration.

To overcome these there are two options, a technologically driven way (ICT e.g. to monitor implementation) and/or applying new means of governance. The latter happens two-fold: addresses of new (stronger) legislations (normally companies) are involved in the legislation procedure as well as other stakeholders that act as "watch dogs" (non-profit associations, NGOs).

Involvement of the first often leads to agreements between the government and the addressees to make regulations by law obsolete and to shift parts of monitoring to the addressees (to control with ICT's by the government and - depending on FOI-regulations - also by citizens and third-sector associations). Monitoring and control depend on information.

When asked to choose the most important of four benefits of e-government, results show 36 percent said it would make government more accountable; 23 percent said it would provide greater information access; 21 percent said it would make government for efficient and cost-effective; and 13 percent said the best benefit would be services that are more convenient.

However, electronic voting requires advanced technological features in order to secure anonymity and authentication at the same time. On the one hand, voters have to identify without any doubt and there must be no way for a person to vote twice.

These problems will remove in the new system by giving much more attention in this.

4.4

Expectation of the people

There is lots of expectation of the people in the society.

"Prosperity of the Economy and Society": This dimension refers to the general socio-economic well being of society. It will create a good economical condition, including relative peace in the world, integration progressing well, and positive moves towards social cohesion and equity.

"Power of Government": This dimension refers to the role of government in people's lives. The main power will be the power of the common people.

"Grade of innovation of information technology": This dimension refers to the development of information technology and its involvement in the politics. This is a dynamic development and diffusion with full speed ahead.

4.3

Transparency and Happiness

For GNH, good governance has categorized under four basic dimensions:

1. Effective government

2. Democratic culture

3. Public participation and efficient voting and

4. Corruption

1. Effective government

The dimensions of efficient government can be measured by various components like overall direction of the government; performance of the central government in delivering services; performance of the judiciary in rendering justice; and performances of leaders at dzongkhag and gewog levels.

 The overall direction of the government is measured by asking the respondents to rate whether the government is going in the right or wrong direction. 85.9% (N=813) agreed the government is going in the right direction, while only 7.9% disagreed.

The reasons for the latter are the anxiety of transition to democratic government, corruption associated with politicians, and the diminishing role of His Majesty the King in governance. Mostly those respondents who reported there is corruption and who are dissatisfied with the functioning of the central government express these. For instance, out of 534 respondents who reported corruption is common in the country, 9% reported that the government is going in the wrong direction.

Similarly, out of 43 respondents who reported dissatisfaction with the functioning of the central ministries, 23.3% reported government is going in the wrong direction.

Concerning the overall performance of the central government in the 12 months preceding the survey, respondents asked to rate different services provided by the central government as excellent, good and poor. Though majority of the respondents reported services like education, health and protecting environment as excellent, services like providing electricity, road, creating job and reducing gap between rich and poor rated poor.

Rural respondents in lower income reported dissatisfaction with the provision of electricity and roads more. For instance, 16.6% and 15.8% (N=791) of the rural respondents with annual household income of less than Nu. 50,000 mentioned central government as poor in providing electricity and road respectively. On the other hand, urban respondents with higher income reported central government as poor in terms of creating employment and reducing income gap. For instance, 25.8% and 19.5% (N=159) of urban respondents with income above Nu. 50,000 reported central government as poor in reducing gap between rich and poor and in creating job respectively.

This problem will not be available in the system of Raj Subramanian. The Government will be effective, transparent and will not be able to work against common people's opinion.

2. Democratic culture

The Economist's Democracy index measures whether countries are full democracies (scores of 8-10), flawed democracies (scores of 6-7.9), hybrid regimes (scores of 4-5.9) and authoritarian regimes (scores below 4) by focusing on five general categories: free and fair election process; civil liberties; functioning of government; political participation; and political culture. In the democracy index of 167 countries in January 2007, Sweden is on the top with 9.88, Iceland is second with 9.71, India is 35th with 7.68, Bhutan is 147th with 2.62, Laos is 155th with 2.10, and North Korea is at the bottom with 1.03. This index grouped 28 countries as functioning democracies, 54 countries as flawed democracies, 30 countries as hybrid regime and 55 countries as authoritarian regimes. As emphasized by His Majesty the King, democracy is more than political parties and elections. It is about ideals, values, and principles of democracy.

Different cultural people may have different opinion, but firstly they are human and first concern of any people is the concern for their family. Therefore, everyone will be happy with this system as the first concern of this system is Human.

3. Public participation and efficient voting

The concept of E-democracy that we put forward based on parallel tracks - Public Participation and Efficient Voting. The use of new technologies to cast a vote in an election is mainly a question of having the required technology in place to offer people the service of online voting alongside other online services. An e-government that includes e-democracy therefore holds out the promise of opportunities for the development of society and the enrichment of democracy.

However, it will only succeed if new technology widely used and trusted. People must want and be able to use new technologies. In order to achieve that, there are some strategic challenges that, in our view, must overcome before success can ensured. In a number of aspects are these preconditions the same as for e-government in general.

The use of new technologies in between elections is a much more complex issue than simply having the appropriate technology in place. It is about creating new relationships between government, in its widest sense, and citizens - opening up new democratic channels through which people can participate in representative democracy.

The new process of Raj Subramanian is the process for public, so they must vote for their favorite candidate and will keep their participation up.

4. Corruption

Corruption essentially means "impairment of integrity, virtue, or moral principle; depravity, decay, inducement to wrong by improper or unlawful means (as bribery), a departure from the original or from what is pure or correct and/or an agency or influence that corrupts." Generally, a public official for private gain considers corruption as abuse of power.

A system that is transparent and accountable, and committed to controlling corruption, is a fundamental feature of good governance and democracy. In order to measure perception of corruption in the country, respondents asked, "In your opinion, how common is corruption in the country?" 56% (N=949) reported that it was common. Similarly when asked, "How many civil servants do you think are involved in corruption?" 58.4% (N=944) reported a few and 22.7% reported most of the civil servants. About the trends of corruption in the country, 44% reported that it increased over the past five years and 16% reported that it remained same in the country.

In the system of Raj Subramanian, there is no chance of corruption as it will be very transparent system. Citizen engagement may be undertaken at all stages of the policy or project development process and is an iterative process that continually infuses citizens' priorities in policy making/project implementation.

4.4

Future of the Voting

It may not be necessary to present physically to give a vote in future. It may be just a matter of click.

Legislating by referendum is not direct democracy, but rather a device used by a representative government to submit a measure to the electorate for an up-or-down vote. As a result, politicians control the process, which they continually limit or corrupt. More fundamentally, the structure of representative government keeps citizens in civic adolescence.

In order to strengthen the effectiveness of the existing legal rights of access to information held by public authorities, citizens should have the right to have that information that is electronically stored, provided to them in electronic form.

4.5

Conclusion

The scenario method offers the opportunity to describe different futures and to try to understand what might happen under the framework of specific variables.

The scenarios partly include inputs that normally might not happen but generally spoken cannot include all these possibilities (e.g. a terrorist attack or a new disease). Nevertheless, they are fruitful to understand many circumstances and framework conditions under which something can happen or not. Therefore, it is no wonder that one pattern that repeats under all scenarios, and therefore concluded as "robust". This is the social demand for information delivery and the technical support in the way of sophisticated information and knowledge management systems. This can see as the counterweight to the increasing influence of the industrial sector on policy-making. Transparency is an integral part of the security of voting systems. It is vital that technology not allowed eroding that transparency.

Not only must the technology itself implement measures to ensure that it is trustworthy - which, in the current technological climate, means voter varied paper ballots - but the system must be managed in a transparent, non-partisan way.

Figure: United nation by E-democracy

The new nation will be a citizen panel where a continuous exchange of information and experience among participants and experts will organize.

This development has supported by such factors as greater influence of social movements, new methods of direct democracy, wider use of consensus-building mechanisms, and new forms of e-enabled democratic political organization. New technological mediation tools and the Internet, in particular, may prove vital in rethinking conceptions of democratic governance. However, only modest democratic gains can be achieve through electronic means, unless a radical redesign of democratic institutions is accomplished, which is not foreseeable in the immediate future.

The new idea of E Democracy will be truly:

By the People

Of the People And

For the People

By accepting the new rule or system of Raj Subramanian, you can change the world and take your own decision or you can wait for the decision of present system. All is in your hand...

References:

1. www.experientia.com/**edemocracy**/
2. http://www.metagovernment.org/wiki/Collaborative_governance
3. http://www.debate.org/debates/Edemocracy-properly-structured-should-replace-Representative-Democracy-everywhere./1/
4. http://www.apaulin.com/research/2010fb/zhupa
5. http://www.twitter.com/edemocracyworld
6. http://www.rajsubramanian.com
7. http://www.facebook.com/edemocracyworld
8. http://en.wikipedia.org/wiki/E-democracy
9. http://democracy.nationalforum.com.au/
10. http://www-01.ibm.com/industries/government/ieg/pdf/e-democracy%20putting%20down%20roots.pdf
11. http://conferences.arts.usyd.edu.au/viewpaper.php?id=122&cf=3
12. http://www.kta.on.ca/KTA_site_RVSD/pdf/cg6.pdf
13. https://evoting.rbs.com/evoting/go
14. http://www.ega.ee/files/edemo_0.pdf